Original title:
The Heart of the Tropics

Copyright © 2025 Creative Arts Management OÜ
All rights reserved.

Author: Hugo Fitzgerald
ISBN HARDBACK: 978-1-80581-678-2
ISBN PAPERBACK: 978-1-80581-205-0
ISBN EBOOK: 978-1-80581-678-2

Harmony in the Hibiscus

In the garden, flowers sway,
Bees are buzzing, come what may.
A squirrel steals a mango snack,
Then tumbles down, what a knack!

Laughter echoes through the trees,
Monkeys dance, a lively breeze.
Lizards sunbathe, flash their style,
While parrots chat and crack a smile.

Petals flutter, colors bright,
Chasing shadows, pure delight.
Neighbors argue who's the best,
Is it hibiscus? You can guess!

All around, the fun is shared,
Nature's joys, we're all impaired.
With a giggle, life unfolds,
In this paradise of gold.

The Lush Embrace of Nature

Coconuts drop, a rolling game,
Watch your head, it's not the same!
A parrot squawks, 'What's for lunch?'
Tropical fruit? Join the bunch!

In the shade, a turtle naps,
While crickets plan their little raps.
A frog named Fred wears fancy shoes,
Who knew style was in the blues?

The sunbeams play like tiny kids,
Flirting softly with the bids.
Everyone's in a merry whirl,
Nature's dance, a joyful twirl!

But wait, a crab walks in with flair,
Strutting by without a care.
We laugh, we cheer, what a show,
In this place where giggles grow!

Shadows Cast by Ferns

Beneath the fronds, a secret place,
Where shadows weave a funny space.
A raccoon's peek, a slow reveal,
Stealing snacks, what a deal!

The ferns are whispering in jest,
"Hide your treasure, that's the best!"
A butterfly joins in the spree,
Wings aflutter, all can see.

A turtle jokes about his pace,
"Slow and steady wins the race!"
While lizards mock his clumsy style,
They wiggle and laugh for a while.

With a chuckle, the wind joins in,
Nature's laughter, a cheeky grin.
In this lush, green, happy land,
Every creature lends a hand!

Journey Through Cinnamon Trails

On cinnamon paths, we stroll with glee,
Fragrant wonders, come smell the spree.
A dog named Max leads the way,
Chasing spices 'till the end of day.

A spice that jumps, a cinnamon twist,
Got to dance with every mist!
A monkey swings down for a chat,
"Hey, you've got quite the hat!"

Beneath the trees, we take a break,
Sipping juice, our thirst to quake.
"Is this sweet?" a critter pokes,
Laughter erupts, oh how it chokes!

With every step, we giggle more,
Nature's jokes we can't ignore.
In this place of laughter bright,
Life's a journey, what a sight!

Exquisite Harmony of Land and Sea

On sunny shores where crabs do dance,
The seagulls squawk, they take a chance.
They steal your fries right off your plate,
And leave you staring, eyes wide as fate.

Drunken palm trees sway in glee,
They throw a shade party, oh so free!
While coconuts cheer, 'We're here to stay!'
And you just hope they won't fall your way.

Sandcastles rise like artful dreams,
But tides come in with mischievous schemes.
You build and laugh, then jump in fright,
As waves crash in to steal your sight.

At sunset, crabs wear shades so cool,
While fish show off their aquatic school.
In this wild blend, all are a part,
A goofy symphony from the sea's heart.

Unraveling the Mystical Understory

In leafy jungles, monkeys play,
With antics that brighten the day.
They're plotting heists on snack packs bold,
While parrots squawk gossip that's pure gold.

Sloths hang low, with style so slow,
In the race for lunch, they steal the show.
Beneath the helm of a viney cape,
A turtle dreams of an ocean escape.

Frogs in costumes leap with cheer,
In search of bugs, they're pioneers!
They croak in harmony, quite the crew,
Could there be a talent show coming too?

With sunlight filtering through tall trees,
The laughter echoes with the breeze.
In nature's jest, we're all a part,
A funny twist, a cheeky art.

The Melody of Tropical Twilights

As the sun dips low, the colors swirl,
Fireflies begin their nightly twirl.
They flicker like stars, a dance divine,
While cicadas hum their silly line.

The palm trees whisper tales so tall,
Of midnight feasts in the moonlight's call.
A crab serenades with a click and a clack,
And the turtles nod, never holding back!

With every splash, the night ignites,
As laughter echoes through balmy nights.
The stars in awe at our joyful zest,
A comedic show that never takes rest.

In the twilight's glow, we sway and spin,
With goofy grins that draw you in.
This melody plays in rhythmic delight,
In the wild harmony of a tropic night.

Ocean's Breath Among Tropical Isles

On soft sandy shores, where the ocean grins,
Shells teem with stories, where adventure begins.
The jellyfish wave with whimsical flair,
While sunburnt tourists forget their care.

With each splash and crash, seagulls descend,
They steal your snacks like a fickle friend.
As waves roll in with a playful tease,
You dodge water's antics like expert athletes!

Coconut drinks topped with paper straws,
Make you feel fancy, without a pause.
But watch for falling fruits from above,
A conch shell smashing is no sign of love!

In quiet coves where the beach meets fate,
You find new friends, both feathered and straight.
With laughter shared in evening's embrace,
The ocean's breath brings a funny grace.

Dances Beneath the Canopy

Monkeys swing with sassy flair,
Parrots gossip in the air.
Lizards bask on sunlit stones,
While frogs croak out their funny tones.

Palm trees sway with silly glee,
As squirrels play a game of 'see'.
The breeze brings laughter, light, and fun,
In a dance beneath the blazing sun.

Coconuts drop with a playful thud,
As children leap, shouting, 'Oh, what a stud!'
The floor's a jungle, wild and bright,
Where every critter is a dance delight.

So grab a friend, don't be shy,
Join the fun as the hours fly.
In this leafy realm, we'll spin and twirl,
Beneath the canopy, give it a whirl!

Secrets of the Emerald Jungle

In emerald thick, the secrets lay,
Whispers of creatures that laugh and play.
A sloth with shades, so laid-back cool,
Every day's a holiday, that's the rule!

The toucan sports a beak, quite grand,
While the jaguar pranks on banana land.
Each critter hides a story or two,
In this vibrant scene, there's mischief to pursue.

A tree frog sings a silly tune,
Dancing 'round the golden cocoon.
Secrets shared with every swing,
Nature's humor makes our hearts sing.

With giggles and joy, the sun peeks through,
The jungle's alive, it's true, it's true!
So come on down, join the spree,
Unlock the secrets, come dance with me!

Where Vibrant Colors Blossom

In fields of hues, the fun unfolds,
With petals bright as stories told.
A butterfly flutters, wearing a crown,
As giggling bees buzz around town.

In gardens lush, where colors collide,
The blooms all boast of their grand pride.
A blooming daisy, with a wink and cheer,
Tells jokes so funny, you'll want to stay near.

Poppies sway, with rhythm and rhyme,
They dance each day, keeping perfect time.
With every gust, a tickle's found,
In a patch of joy, spinning round and round.

So let us skip through this lively scene,
With blossoms bright, forever green.
Where laughter blooms in full array,
In vibrant colors, come join the play!

Echoes of the Island Song

On shores where laughter meets the sea,
A song arises, wild and free.
Shells hum tunes, sandy feet tap,
Jellyfish dance, napping in their wrap.

The coconut crabs, with pincers swift,
Provide the rhythm, a clumsy gift.
Seagulls add a squawky cheer,
As fish join in, splashing near.

With a conch shell blowing a silly beat,
The island's alive with joy and heat.
Waves play along, in jolly refrain,
As laughter echoes, again and again.

So come and sway with the island's hum,
In this paradise, we're never glum.
With every note that floats our way,
We'll celebrate life, come what may!

Hues of Life in Abundant Canopies

In a jungle gym of green, they play,
Caterpillars dance, thinking it's ballet.
Parrots squawk in polka-dot flair,
While monkeys practice their circus air.

Leaves gossip secrets in rustling tones,
With vines that giggle on lazy stones.
Bouncing berries wear hats of delight,
As they roll down hills, oh what a sight!

High above, a sloth checks the score,
Too slow to catch up, it's back for more.
Bees gossip sweetly, it's quite the scene,
In this leafy nook where laughter's the queen.

Sunshine and shadows share a light pun,
While critters conspire to out-run the sun.
Every branch has a story to tell,
In a silly world where all's gone well.

Dappled Light on the Forest Floor

Sunbeams scatter like giggles in flight,
A squirrel in shades says, "I'm feeling bright!"
Leaves laugh softly, creating a song,
While mushrooms wobble, playing along.

A fern twirls its fronds, oh what a tease,
While beetles march as if on parade, please!
Underfoot, the moss thickens the plot,
Where snails play poker and moss takes their slot.

Rabbits in sneakers hop through the grime,
They race with the shadows, just wasting time.
Even the toadstools whisper with glee,
In this quirky realm where we're all carefree.

A dappled world where surprises abound,
With each tiny creature, a laugh can be found.
Sunlight and giggles merge in a swirl,
On this forest floor, watch the fun unfurl.

Rhythm of the Tidal Heart

Waves clap hands on the sandy shore,
In sync with the seagulls' raucous roar.
Crabs in disco hats do their best strut,
While fish flaunt tails, making a cut.

The ocean winks, a cheeky old sprite,
Tides bumbling in, what a hilarious sight!
Starfish practice their best dance moves,
As jellyfish jiggle and try to improve.

Beachcombers chuckle, collecting their finds,
Shells wear grins, with nature that binds.
A sandcastle prince gives a royal wave,
While seahorses swim, the kings of the brave.

The tides have a rhythm, an offbeat cheer,
As barnacles giggle, oh dear, oh dear!
In this salty haven, let laughter be our art,
As life rolls in waves, with a rhythmic heart.

A Palette of Nature's Warmth

Colors spill out like paint gone wild,
A chameleon grins, oh, it's beguiled!
Bright blooms gossip, in shades they flaunt,
While butterflies argue who's the best flaunt.

Sunsets smirk in purple and gold,
As fireflies twinkle, their stories unfold.
Bumblebees hum their sweet little tune,
While ladybugs roll like it's afternoon.

A colorful chaos, a joyful mess,
In every hue, there's laughter to express.
Birds paint the sky with their bright little calls,
In nature's gallery, where wonder never stalls.

Under this canvas, the world's a hoot,
With melodies danced in flora's own suit.
So let's splash our lives with giggles and art,
This vibrant world, oh, it stole my heart!

The Sorcery of Mango-Sweet Skies

In mango trees, the laughter beams,
A dancing bee with ice cream dreams.
The sun winks down with a playful tease,
While parrots squawk their rhymes with ease.

A coconut falls, a surprise in the buns,
Rolling on paths, oh what a pun!
Frisky monkeys swing with flair,
Chasing each other without a care.

The breeze plays hide-and-seek with hats,
As lizards sunbathe on welcome mats.
A hammock sways, inviting a snooze,
But watch out for friends with playful ruse!

With vibrant hues, the sunsets dance,
In this place, we all take a chance.
For laughter blooms with the flowers' spread,
Come join the fun, no mind to dread!

Ephemeral Moments in Nature's Clutch

Tickling leaves when the breezes sigh,
Crabs scuttle sideways, oh me, oh my!
Catching that moment, like catching a cold,
With fishy tales that never get old.

The clouds shape-shift like cotton candy,
Eagles swoop down, feeling quite dandy.
A game of tag with the rays of the sun,
The day races off, but oh, was it fun!

Palm trees canoodle with horizons wide,
While waves whisper secrets with every tide.
Flip-flops abandon, left in the sand,
As laughter erupts, completely unplanned.

Chasing the fireflies, oh what a sight,
Joking about who could catch the most bright.
In fleeting moments, we savor the glee,
For life's little quirks make us truly free!

Cerulean Skies Over Tropical Dreams

Beneath a sky painted in playful blue,
A curious goat bids the clouds adieu.
Flip-flops squeak on the soft sandy floor,
And sunburned noses beg for one day more.

The tides laugh hard, splashing out grins,
While seagulls argue about who wins.
A child's kite tangles in a palm tree's hair,
The coconut laughs, saying life's unfair!

Drifting on seas where sunrays pool,
Fish throw a party, it's the new cool.
Laughter erupts in a splashy embrace,
As mermaids giggle, enjoying the race.

As twilight whispers, and stars softly gleam,
We toast to the gold of our sun-drenched dream.
With hearts full of joy and a tinge of cream,
We dance 'til the moon starts to intervene!

Enchanted Reflections in Still Waters

Ripples weave stories that tickle the mind,
As frogs croak symphonies, humor entwined.
Butterflies flip with a flair, what a show!
Reflecting our giggles, the water must know.

The turtles lazily pose, taking their time,
While fish flash past, like a slapstick mime.
A splash from a duck, a quack and a chase,
Nature's own jester, oh what a place!

Bamboo stands tall, swaying with pride,
As dragonflies dance, and the frogs do a slide.
Footprints in mud tell tales of our spree,
While we make a mess of our wild jubilee.

In twilight's embrace, we count every star,
Making wishes on laughter, near and far.
With hearts full of joy, we dip our toes,
In enchanted reflections, where merriment flows!

Vibrant Sanctuary of Beasts and Birds

In the jungle, monkeys swing,
Chasing tails, they dance and sing.
Parrots squawk in loud debate,
Is it breakfast? Oh, it's late!

Sloths are hanging, looking cool,
While iguanas break all rules.
The jaguar rolls, sun-tanned chic,
Can't remember, is it peek-a-boo this week?

A toucan's beak, a rainbow hue,
Came for lunch, who knew it grew?
The creatures laugh, they prance about,
In this haven, fun's no doubt!

Each morning's filled with crazy sights,
A party starts at dawn's first light.
This vibrant place, oh what a show,
With beasts and birds, the fun won't slow!

Tapestry of Colorful Lives

In the market, fruits collide,
Mangoes blush, and lemons hide.
Soursop whispers sweet delight,
While coconuts play peek-a-boo at night.

Chickens laugh as they run around,
In a dance of chaos, no one's bound.
Lizards flaunt their green parade,
In sunlit spots, their charm displayed.

The beach is where the colors blend,
With sunsets that seem to never end.
Painted skies, a melting dream,
Where every shade bursts at the seam!

In this patchwork, life's a fest,
A vibrant scene that's simply the best.
So gather 'round, embrace the cheer,
For in this land, fun's always near!

Dreamscapes of Flamboyant Flora

Petals whisper in the breeze,
Swaying softly, they aim to tease.
Carnivorous plants, a funny view,
"Dinner's served!" they call to you.

The orchids flaunt their purple crowns,
While lilies wear their velvet gowns.
In this garden, laughter grows,
As tulips tell their silly woes.

Banana trees bend, a bending grace,
Chasing shadows, a funny race.
Cacti chuckle, arms out wide,
"Come join us, this is our pride!"

From every leaf, a story spins,
Of tangled roots and leafy twins.
In dreamscapes bright, let spirits soar,
Flamboyant wonders, forever more!

The Soft Caress of a Coastal Kiss

Waves tickle toes on sandy shores,
The ocean giggles, laughter roars.
Seagulls squawk with cheeky grace,
As crabs perform their sideways race.

Umbrella hats in vibrant shades,
Cover snickering in sunlit glades.
The sandcastles bravely stand tall,
Until the waves decide to brawl.

Shells gather stories, secrets rare,
Each tide brings tales of ocean fare.
With laughter shared and joy run free,
This coastal life is pure esprit!

So bring your friends and some cold drinks,
Let's toast to all the fun, just think!
In this bliss, silly moments sway,
The soft caress, come out to play!

Curves of Paradise on Distant Horizons

On shores where coconuts tumble and play,
A crab's got his moves, he's here to stay.
He dances on sand with a wobbly beat,
Stealing my flip-flops, oh what a feat!

The sun is a friend who won't leave you be,
While I sip on my drink, oh so carefree.
With waves that giggle and tickle my toes,
Who knew the ocean had joking flows?

A parrot's advice? It's quite the surprise,
Telling me secrets with glittering eyes.
He squawks for a snack, then takes to the sky,
As I drop my sandwich and start to cry!

But laughter erupts as the fish start to dance,
In this bright little haven, come take a chance.
With sights that confound and jokes that won't stop,
I'll stay till the sun says it's time for a swap!

A Tantalizing Breeze from Paradise

A breeze comes a-whistling through palm fronds and vines,
Whispering secrets and punchlines in lines.
It teases my hair like a playful young child,
Saying, "Come on now, let's go run wild!"

With mangoes that giggle and pineapples wink,
I can't help but chuckle and reach for a drink.
The sun's got a grin, it's got jokes up its sleeve,
While I, on the sand, pretend to believe.

But watch out for seagulls who plot heavy theft,
As they plot over snacks, feeling proud and bereft.
I toss them some chips, they laugh with delight,
Stolen joy as they fly into the light.

The warmth wraps me up in a blanket of glee,
This paradise breeze is like a good cup of tea.
With laughter and giggles that dance through the air,
Who knew such a trip would be beyond compare!

Soft Footfalls in the Jungle's Heart

With soft little footfalls, I roam through the shade,
Where monkeys throw parties, and sloths serenade.
A vine swings me 'round like a carnival ride,
I giggle and whirl, feeling joy as my guide.

But what's that ahead, moving low in the grass?
A lizard who sunbathes, he's got quite the sass.
He tells me to chill, take it easy, my friend,
While he sprawls in the sun, saying, "Time to transcend!"

The toucans are painting the sky with their wings,
While trees clap their branches and sway as they sing.
A turtle chimes in with a rhythm so slow,
Teasing me gently to just take it slow.

The creatures are lively, they dance and they prance,
In this jungle soirée, there's always a chance.
To swap jokes with a toucan, or play leapfrog with smiles,

This soft-footed journey makes all life worthwhile!

Color Splash of Tropical Mornings

Awake to the colors, it's a painter's delight,
With oranges and pinks that burst into sight.
The roosters are laughing, they crow with such flair,
While I try for coffee, but spill everywhere!

Papayas are giggling, they bounce on the trees,
In this cheery, bright Eden, it's all just a tease.
A parakeet joins in with a song and a flap,
Stealing my muffins, oh what a mishap!

A hammock is swaying, it waves me to come,
But first I must dodge the stray coconut drum.
With laughter resounding, and chaos in play,
Tropical mornings are just one big buffet!

So here in the sun, let the joy take its place,
With colors and giggles all over the space.
Rediscover your laughter, let the fun never cease,
In a land full of whimsy, there's always a piece!

Dance of the Colorful Wings

In a land where the breezes play,
Birds wear costumes bright and gay.
They twist and twirl with such delight,
As monkeys cheer, it's quite the sight.

A parrot shimmies, shakes a tail,
While a timid frog joins the trail.
The hummingbird sips a sweet drink,
And winks at all, don't you dare blink!

Butterflies wear their fancy hats,
While chattering squirrels join the spats.
They waltz on petals, golden and true,
Who knew nature could throw such a zoo?

In a show where laughter is king,
Nature's chorus begins to sing.
With flaps and flutters, they all conspire,
To dance and prance, lifting hearts higher.

Serene Waters of the Verdant Isles

By the river where the turtles nap,
Fish do flips, such a splashy clap.
A coconut floats, just taking it slow,
While crabs hold a race, doing a row.

The otters slide down slippery banks,
Chortling loud with jovial pranks.
While frogs face off with a game of leap,
The joyful noise—it's hard to keep.

A heron lifts off with style and grace,
But lands in a puddle—what a disgrace!
While the sun sets with a cheeky grin,
The waters reflect where the fun begins.

In a splash of laughter, the day fades away,
With creatures telling tales till the end of the day.
These playful waters never grow old,
With stories of fun waiting to be told.

Laughter of the Jungle's Spirits

In the depths where the shadows grow,
The pangolins dance with a clumsy flow.
While raccoons sing off-key, quite bold,
Ghosts of the jungle, their tales unfold.

Lianas twist to a rhythm they feel,
As sloths join in; oh, what a meal!
A tiger chuckles, 'I'm fierce, can't you see?'
But falls on a vine, 'Was that really me?'

Monkeys steal hats from tourists who gawk,
While a wise old owl just laughs and squawks.
With rustling leaves and a twinkling eye,
Even the shyest will give it a try.

As moonlight spills on the froggies who croak,
And laughter erupts like some marvelous joke.
In the jungle, where spirits play free,
Every giggle is part of the decree.

Mosaic of Flora and Fauna

Here's a patchwork of colors so bright,
Where flowers strut, putting on a sight.
The daisies giggle, with petals so wide,
While sunflowers grin with the sun as their guide.

Each leaf dances with a whimsical flair,
Swaying along, they throw up their hair.
A dandy little beetle takes a stroll,
In a tuxedo, he plays his role.

Vines whisper secrets behind every tree,
As butterflies flutter, sipping with glee.
The grasshoppers join with a hop and a skip,
Bouncing around with a jubilant grip.

In blooms of laughter, a symphony grows,
Nature's own rhythm, everyone knows.
With a pomp and a flair, life's a fun show,
In this patchwork world where we all glow.

Salt and Spice of Coastal Winds

On the beach, a seagull stole my fries,
I guess he thought they were a tasty prize.
The waves crashed in with a salty cheer,
While I searched for napkins, oh dear, oh dear!

Flip-flops squeaking as I chase that bird,
He squawks away, not caring, so absurd!
Palm trees dancing, what a silly sight,
Nature's own show, an afternoon delight.

My sunburned nose, a bright cherry red,
Reminds me that sunscreen's my only friend.
With fish tacos served on a wobbly plate,
I'm laughing so hard, it must be fate!

Beneath a bright sky, laughter spills like wine,
Life's simple joys, oh they truly shine.
In this coastal land, where the wild things roam,
I found joy and laughter, and called it home.

Temptation of Mango and Coconut

A ripe mango, too juicy to resist,
It slipped from my grip, oh, what a twist!
Down the hill, it rolled without a care,
Chasing that fruit, life's a fun fair.

Coconut breezes tickle my nose,
As I dodge crab traps and dance with toes.
It's a slippery slope, quite literally,
Snack time becomes a sport, you see!

I wrestled with a shell, what a game,
If only these shores knew my name.
With sticky fingers and a goofy grin,
Laughter echoes, let the beach games begin!

Under the sun, I'm the fruit-fumbling champ,
This tropical life is an endless camp.
In the land of coconuts and mango bliss,
Each bite leads to another fruity miss!

Silence Amidst the Mangroves

Amidst the trees, a hermit crab prances,
In his tiny home, he takes his chances.
Whispers of vines, a curious place,
Nature's own giggle fills the space.

I tiptoe softly, a stealthy knight,
But trip on roots, what a funny sight!
The birds overhead chuckle and swoop,
While I'm tangled like a confused loop.

A frog jumps in, makes a splat!
My giggles burst forth, oh imagine that!
With marshy footing and mud on my shoe,
Life's little messes give a colorful hue.

In this green fortress, I find my muse,
Where silence reigns, and I just snooze.
The laughter of life, in every twist,
This mangrove adventure, I can't resist!

Sunlit Pathways Through Thick Green

Sunlight breaks through the leafy crown,
I'm on a journey, but where's the town?
Chasing fireflies in the golden gleam,
I trip on roots, and tumble like a dream.

A squirrel darts past, with a nut so grand,
He knows this path better than planned.
I wave goodbye as he scurries away,
Who knew squirrels could brighten the day?

Bamboo whispers secrets to the breeze,
While I navigate thickets with the greatest of ease.
Every step I take, quirky sounds I glean,
Each rustle and giggle, a lively scene.

In this sunlit maze, I dance without care,
Turning every stumble into a flair.
Through pathways green, I set my feet free,
Finding joy in the journey, just being me!

Tranquility of Tides in Motion

The waves dance like they're on a spree,
Fish doing the cha-cha, oh what glee!
Seagulls crack jokes as they soar so high,
While crabs throw tantrums and wonder why.

An octopus juggling, a sight so rare,
Mermaids giggle, flipping their hair.
Ocean's a circus, with acts so bold,
Even the plankton are laughing, I've been told.

A dolphin with shades, what a cool dude!
Sipping on coconut, in such a good mood.
The tide pulls back, with a chuckle and splash,
As sandcastles melt in a comedic crash.

So come take a dip in this laughter-filled sea,
Where the bubbles of joy set your spirit free!
Amidst all the chaos, the giggles reside,
In this watery playground, there's nowhere to hide.

Lullabies of the Tropical Rain

Pitter patter, the raindrops sing,
As frogs start a choir, what a wild fling!
The trees wear hats, all soaked and proud,
While the puddles giggle, gathering a crowd.

A monkey with rhythm, dances in delight,
Swinging from branches, oh what a sight!
Parrots crack wise, with jokes so bright,
While worms in the soil plan a rain dance tonight.

The thunder joins in, like a big wild cheer,
While ants line up, they've got no fear.
Slipping and sliding, oh what a race,
As the rain keeps on laughing, with cheeky grace.

So let the drops fall, like a happy tune,
In this funny downpour, we'll dance till noon!
Embrace the wet wild, with giggles we gain,
As laughter and raindrops wash away pain.

The Golden Touch of Sunlit Sands

The sun spills gold, oh what a show,
While sandcastles rise and then sink like snow.
Children giggle, buckets in hand,
Building their dreams in a sandy land.

A crab wears a bucket, as a cool little hat,
Strutting around, now how about that?
The breeze tickles noses, laughter's the plan,
While sunbathers giggle, "Hey, where's my tan?"

Seashells gossip, they have tales to share,
Of long-lost treasures and who's the best pair.
Kites dip and dive, they're joy on a string,
While a dog rolls over, 'Oh, that's the thing!'

So bask in the sun, let your worries float,
On waves of giggles, let joy be your boat.
Sand between toes, the world is so grand,
Come join in the fun on this sunlit strand.

Majestic Whispers of the Wind

The wind tells tales of a bird in flight,
With whispers so soft, that tickle the night.
Trees sway and shimmy, a dance in the air,
While leaves drop down as if they don't care.

A kite gets zany, it's off on a spree,
Chasing its dreams, as wild as can be!
The clouds start a giggle, then rumble with might,
"Catch us if you can!" they call in delight.

Fluffy as marshmallows, they drift and they roam,
While the wind sings a tune of its breezy home.
Coconuts roll, staggering with flair,
"Watch out!" they exclaim, "We're going somewhere!"

So listen to whispers, with a grin on your face,
In this wind-blown world, we all share this space.
Let laughter take flight, in this free-spirited race,
For in nature's embrace, there's joy we can trace.

The Call of the Singing River

A river gurgles with delight,
It hums a tune both day and night.
Fish dance beneath in silly rows,
While frogs croak choruses, heaven knows.

With every splash, a chuckle flows,
The water tickles all it knows.
The banks burst forth with colors bright,
As dragonflies wear hats of light.

A hippo giggles, splashing through,
Says, "Wish you could swim, but I know you!"
The ducks parade, their feathers preen,
In this silly place, the joy is seen.

Oh, singing river, bring your cheer,
We'll splash and laugh, forget our fear.
For as long as we can wade and play,
We'll dance in water, come what may.

Serenity Amongst the Timid Twilights

In twilight's hush, the stars peek shy,
The fireflies flicker, oh my oh my!
A crab on the shore does the cha-cha dance,
While shy little lizards take a glance.

The moon grins down, a curious guest,
With shadows playing hide and jest.
A parrot giggles, "What a sight!"
As night slips in, avoiding the fright.

The sound of coconuts falling near,
Each thud like laughter from the sphere.
In timid twilights, we find our cheer,
Beneath the stars, there's nothing to fear.

So let us sway with the gentle breeze,
In silly dreams, we'll do as we please.
For in this warm, whimsical night,
The world's just a stage, everything's right.

Beneath the Stars of Eternal Summer

Stars sprinkle laughter on the bay,
While crickets play their night parade.
A turtle comes with a tired groan,
Says, "Summer's long! Just let me moan!"

Coconuts drop like tiny bombs,
Making waves of giggles and psalms.
A beach ball bounces, lost and found,
While seagulls dive with screeching sound.

The sunfish tosses jokes in the tide,
With every splash, the fun can't hide.
Beneath this sky, oh so blue,
We laugh as if the world's brand new.

So raise your glass of coconut drink,
Let's toast to life, and not to think.
For in the warmth of endless summer,
Laughter thrives in nature's great slumber.

Symphony of the Condor's Flight

High above, the condors glide,
In a waltz that makes the mountains slide.
They flap and twirl in a funny dance,
While the valleys below lead a merry prance.

With every swoop and swirl, they sing,
Echoing through valleys like a funky fling.
"Watch out!" cries an amused old goat,
"Your wardrobe's so loud, it'll surely float!"

Down in the meadow, the critters cheer,
As rustling leaves bring laughter near.
"Join the choir!" a squirrel calls out,
"In this flight of fancy, there's no doubt!"

So let them soar, those feathered jesters,
In their symphony, they are the besters.
In the sky where they make their play,
Life just becomes a bright ballet.

Serenade of the Parrots' Song

Perched on a branch, with flair so bright,
They squawk out jokes from dawn till night.
Colorful gossip in the air they weave,
A comedy club in the jungle's leave.

With beaks like microphones, they take the stage,
A feathered cabaret, the wild turns page.
Comic relief in the leafy expanse,
Who knew that parrots loved to dance?

In coconut hats, they strut their stuff,
Their punchlines sharp, their antics tough.
Sipping on nectar like it's a cocktail,
Laughter rings out, like a vibrant gale.

So next time you wander through green and gold,
Listen closely for stories boldly told.
Those feathered jesters will make you grin,
In their tropical realm, the fun begins!

The Emerald Kiss of Nature's Hand

The canopy whispers secrets of green,
Where vines tussle like kids in a dream.
Leaves waggle their fingers, and giggles ensue,
Bouncing light-heartedly in the morning dew.

Mango trees chuckle, dropping fruit with glee,
While playful lizards dance carefreely.
A sneaky breeze makes the flowers sway,
As if nature's teasing, in a quirky way.

Bananas wear smiles, their peels in a twist,
Coconuts brainstorm, they can't resist.
In this luscious theater, life finds its fun,
Moments of joy in the tropical sun.

So lift up your spirits, embrace the green flash,
Join the wild chorus, let laughter clash.
Nature's embrace is magic indeed,
Where joy grows plentiful, like a vibrant seed!

Roots that Cradle Ancient Stories

Beneath the soil, tales twist and weave,
Roots high-five each other, oh, can you believe?
They chat about rain, the sun, and the floods,
Making history as they suck up the buds.

Old trees gossip of long-lost friends,
A squirrel's adventure where the fun never ends.
With bark that's a library, time's pages unfold,
Funny dialogues of ages retold.

Idling in shadows, critters convene,
Roots sing songs that are evergreen.
The wise old moss offers comedic relief,
While branches crack jokes, beyond belief.

So dig down deep, let curiosity flow,
To find where the roots tell tales that glow.
An embrace of laughter, from the ground to the sky,
Nature's comedy show, oh my, oh my!

Journey to the Island's Heartbeat

On a boat made of laughter, we sail away,
With waves that giggle, letting worries sway.
The sun shares winks, and the breeze throws a grin,
An island adventure where joy won't thin.

Tropical breezes tickle the toes,
While seagulls dive in with silly poses.
Coconut cocktails with hats made of leaves,
Sipping on sunshine, the island deceives.

Crabs in a limbo contest on the shore,
Flip your shell hats and join in the roar.
Palm trees sway, jesters in the sun,
Dancing with style, oh, this trip's number one!

When twilight falls, the fireflies tease,
It's a comedy night, feel the warm breeze.
From sunrise to moonrise, spirits take flight,
In the land of delight, everything feels right!

Stories Carried by Tropical Breezes

A parrot squawks a joke, oh dear,
As mangoes tumble down, have no fear!
Frogs wear hats and dance a jig,
While iguanas groove, each doing a big.

Coconut drinks spill like thoughts on a page,
As wind whispers secrets, setting the stage.
Laughter floats high on a bright sunbeam,
Spreading tales like icing on a dream.

A crab walks sideways, checking his stance,
While monkeys join in for a silly dance.
Palm trees sway, witnessing the glee,
In this breezy land, wild and free!

Even the sun smirks, its light so bold,
While tales tickle hearts, never getting old.
So come, let's laugh with the breeze today,
In this tropical world where jesters play!

Vibrations of Life in the Sunset Glow

Sipping on coconuts, the sun dips low,
Belly laughs echo, stealing the show.
Crickets serenade with a catchy tune,
While fireflies dance 'neath a big, full moon.

Flip-flops squeak as friends race to the sea,
Playing tag like kids, oh such jubilee!
Starfish have parties, waving their arms,
While sea turtles bask, charm in their charms.

A dog in shades lounges on the shore,
While a crab sneezes, and all of us roar.
Sunsets drip orange, a colorful spree,
In this quirky place, pure hilarity!

As night unfolds, laughter lingers near,
With jokes carried off by the pelicans here.
In the glow of dusk, let's enjoy the show,
In this scene of life where fun tends to grow!

Kisses of Dew at Dawn's First Light

Morning creeps up with a giggling breeze,
Dew drops spin tales, fresh as you please.
Roosters make coffee, clucking along,
While flowers wake up to birds' cheery song.

A turtle in slippers tries to outrun,
The sun as it yawns, ready for fun.
Bumblebees splash in pollen's embrace,
While ants form a line in this funny race.

Giggling leaves shiver with morning's tease,
As dew kisses petals, dancing with ease.
A monkey swings high, tossing confetti,
In this dewy morning, oh so ready!

So savor the chuckles as dawn breaks anew,
In this whimsical light, life's joy shines through.
For every new day is a ripe, juicy bite,
Brimming with laughter from morning till night!

A Dance Beneath the Palm Fronds

Palm fronds sway, calling to the beat,
As fish flip in rhythm, oh what a treat!
The sun dons shades, ready to groove,
While waves do the hustle, making us move.

A toucan struts with the flair of a star,
While crabs in tuxedos prepare for the bar.
Salsa of colors, bright and alive,
Each creature joining in, jiving to thrive.

Under the moonlight, the coconuts twirl,
As laughter erupts, a jubilant whirl.
The night brings delight with a hint of tease,
As shadows shimmy among the palm trees.

So shake off your worries and dance with delight,
In this tropical paradise, everything's bright!
For every step taken is a joyful embrace,
In this rhythmic world, let's find our place!

Journeys Beyond the Rain

Raindrops dance like tiny clowns,
Slipping off the vibrant towns.
Umbrellas flipping in a race,
Laughter spills all over the place.

Puddles form a laughing stage,
Each splash a silly, playful page.
With every step the mud does sing,
Riding on a worm, a strange king.

Mangoes drip with sugary flair,
Juicy jokes hang in the air.
Bananas slip, all funny and bright,
Nature's punchlines give us delight.

Lush Vistas of Whispered Memories

Vines twist like a riddle told,
Where secrets wait for hands to hold.
Parrots squawk, a comic show,
Through leafy halls, where forget-me-not grow.

Coffee beans giggle, dark and roasted,
As they brew up tales, coast to coasted.
Breezes whisper in playful tones,
While the monkeys steal the phones!

Picnics planned with sandwiches bold,
Ants in line, so brave and bold.
A grasshopper joins in, leaps and bounds,
Claiming the crown of the funny sounds.

Twilight Tales of Coastal Retreat

As sun dips down with a wink and sigh,
Seagulls tell jokes as they fly high.
Shells laugh softly on the beach,
While the sunset tries hard to reach.

Flip-flops stumble, oh what a sight!
Feet caught in sand, a silly fight.
Tide pools bubble with stories of fish,
While crabs tap dance, fulfilling a wish.

Bonfires crackle, marshmallows roast,
'Round the fire, laughter is the host.
Ghost stories flutter, with giggles in between,
Making even the spooky seem almost serene.

Spirals of History in Ancient Trees

Trees wear their age like a badge of cheer,
Whispering secrets for all to hear.
Branches bend like a wise old man,
Telling tales of an ancient plan.

Roots tangle like a silly dance,
In the shade, give time a chance.
Knots and gnarls, a face so funny,
Woodpeckers drum, all things quite punny.

Squirrels plot with mischievous schemes,
Hiding their spoils like treasure dreams.
Under the cover of green we roam,
Claiming the woods, a laughter-filled home.

Echoes of Rainforest Rhythms

In the jungle, monkeys swing,
A dance party, they're the king.
Parrots squawk a cheerful tune,
Guess they're aiming for a cartoon.

The sloths lounge like it's a dream,
In hammocks made of jungle seam.
Lizards sneak a peek, oh my!
It's a rave beneath the sky!

Frogs croak beats, they're quite the band,
While beetles clap with little hands.
Swinging vines take to the stage,
Nature's concert, all the rage!

With every stomp and every cheer,
The rainforest holds its breath near.
So let the rhythms never part,
It's jungle fever, pure heart!

Vibrant Blooms Beneath the Sky

Flowers flaunt their colors bright,
In a beauty contest, oh, what a sight!
With petals waving in the breeze,
They gossip like they know the keys.

Sunflowers seem to know the score,
While roses blush and ask for more.
Lilies wear their crowns with pride,
While daisies giggle on the side.

Bees buzz in their tiny suits,
As if they're hitting fashion roots.
They sip the nectar like fine wine,
In this wild floral spin and twine!

So here's to blooms that cheer and prance,
In colors bright, they love to dance.
Each petal whispers a happy song,
In the garden where we all belong!

Beneath the Canopy's Embrace

In the shade where critters play,
A squirrel steals a snack today.
Who's the thief? The parrot squawks,
While monkeys giggle from the rocks.

Sunbeams sneak through leafy green,
As if they're searching for the scene.
Tigers yawn and stretch with grace,
Claiming every cozy space.

Down below, the ants parade,
In tiny boots, they're quite displayed.
With leaves as banners, they march tall,
In a tiny, bustling carnival!

Underneath the leafy dome,
All creatures feel right at home.
With every rustle and every call,
The canopy's the life of all!

Tropic Dreams in Luminescent Nights

When the moonlight starts to shine,
The fireflies create a line.
Dancing in the warm, sweet air,
They flirt with dreams without a care.

Crickets sing their evening tunes,
While owls hoot with silly boons.
A playful breeze joins in the fun,
Underneath the twinkling run.

Stars above drop by to peek,
At the antics of the sleek.
With laughter shared amongst the trees,
The night becomes a gentle tease.

In this world where dreams run wild,
Every heart is free, beguiled.
So let us dance till morning light,
In tropic dreams that feel just right!

Nectar and Nectarine Dreams

In the orchard where the fruit swings,
Bees hum songs on sticky wings.
Juicy laughter drips from trees,
Dreams of nectar in the breeze.

Sunshine wriggles in a dance,
Fuzzy peaches, a sweet romance.
Sipping juice, we take a ride,
On a fruit-flavored, joyful tide.

Ants throw parties under the shade,
Sipping nectar, they parade.
Chasing vibes, oh what a sight!
In the orchard's pure delight.

So raise a glass, my fruity friends,
Let's feast till the golden light ends.
In a world where sweet dreams bloom,
Laughter grows in every room.

Symphonies of the Wild

In the jungle, a concert starts,
Monkeys strum on hidden hearts.
A gibbon swings with flair and grace,
Singing tunes in a furry embrace.

Parrots squawk in bright display,
Dancing leaves join in the fray.
Caterpillars tap their feet,
Creating rhythms oh so sweet.

Lemurs twirl like feathers in air,
While crocs just grin, with a wild stare.
Beetles march, a band so bold,
In this symphony, joy unfolds.

With every giggle under the sun,
Nature's choir has just begun.
So let's laugh with all our might,
In the woods of pure delight.

Beneath the Blanket of Green

Under the vines where giggles grow,
Laughter sprouts, and breezes blow.
A hammock swings, as frogs play tunes,
While flowers dance beneath the moons.

The sun slips in with a silly grin,
Kissing leaves, where fun begins.
Bouncing butterflies, a clumsy jest,
Float over petals, on a joyful quest.

Chikadees chirp, their voices loud,
Telling jokes to a dancing crowd.
Lizards slip wearing sun hats too,
Charming all in their vibrant view.

So join the revels in the green,
Where laughter's woven in every scene.
Beneath the leaves, we'll play and roam,
In this jungle, we find our home.

Cascades of Joyful Laughter

Waterfalls giggle over rocks,
While turtles float, acting in flocks.
Sunlight sprays like playful mist,
Kites dance, in the air, they twist.

Down by the stream, frogs make a splash,
With every jump, they cause a crash.
Otters slide with glee, so slick,
In this place, fun's the magic trick.

Drifting leaves make a merry choir,
As laughter echoes, never tire.
Splashing friends in a joyful race,
In the water, we find our place.

Let's dive deep and take the leap,
In giggles, spirits, we shall keep.
Under cascades, where we all play,
Joyful moments brighten our day.

The Pulse of a Tropical Dawn

The sun pops up like a surprised toast,
Birds chirp loud, like they're bragging the most.
Palm trees sway as they dance to the beat,
While lizards scramble for breakfast to eat.

A coconut falls, it gives quite a thud,
A squirrel dashes, looking for nuts in the mud.
The world wakes up with a giggle and cheer,
As the day begins with a splash of good beer!

The mangoes are ripe, just hanging around,
Like they too, want to dance on the ground.
The breeze tickles noses, it's playful and spry,
While iguanas pose, thinking they're shy.

So here we are, under skies oh so bright,
In a land of delight, from day to the night.
With laughter and chaos, the day rolls along,
In this tropical realm, we all sing our song.

Serenity in the Shade

Beneath big leaves where the cool breezes flow,
A monkey swings by, putting on quite a show.
It's naptime for sloths, who hang with great grace,
While the ants march in line, all keeping their pace.

A hammock invites for a lazy retreat,
But watch out for frogs trying to take your seat!
The lizards are sunbathing, basking with pride,
As the world spins along on its merry ride.

A parrot squawks tales of old island lore,
While ducks form a band, and they try to encore.
With all of this fun, it's the chaos of calm,
Where the wild and the silly mix freely with charm.

So sip on your drink with a slice of fresh lime,
And toast to the breeze, for it knows how to rhyme.
In this jungle of laughter, we revel and play,
Finding joy in the shade, come what may!

Petals in the Paradise

Flowers bloom bright, like they just won the game,
They wink at the bees, who all know their fame.
Butterflies float with a flair of delight,
As they rate each petal, from morning to night.

A garden parade of colors and scents,
Where each flower struts with major intents.
The marigolds giggle, the orchids make jokes,
While tulips gossip, giving the pansies pokes.

A breeze rushes in, like an uninvited guest,
Knocking blossoms around; it thinks it's the best!
But the flowers all laugh, they won't take a dive,
For they bloom even brighter, proving they thrive.

So let's dance through the petals, forget all the fuss,
With colors and laughter, there's plenty for us.
In this cheerful patch, the joy never fades,
As we twirl through the blooms, and waddle like shades.

Moonlit Tides and Starry Nights

The moon hangs low, it's a big, goofy clown,
Waves lap the shore, trying to pull us down.
Stars giggle softly, playing peek-a-boo,
While the night crabs scurry, all up in their cue.

The beach is a stage; oh the drama unfolds,
As the fish in the sea share tales that are bold.
The wind joins the fun, with whispers and sighs,
Tickling the night with its sneaky surprise.

A tourist flips flops, gets caught in the sand,
While dolphins jump high, waving their fin hand.
Under this blanket of shimmering light,
Every wave tells a story, both silly and bright.

With coconuts clinking in tropical cheer,
The laughter of friends is what we hold dear.
So let's raise our cups to the warmth of the night,
In this magical realm, everything feels right.

Rainfall's Melody on Leafy Roofs

Pitter, patter, drops do play,
On leafy roofs, they laugh all day.
The gutters sing a silly tune,
While frogs join in, under the moon.

Umbrellas dance, they spin and twirl,
As watchful birds around them whirl.
A parrot squawks, a funny jest,
While puddles form, the world's a fest.

Splashing feet in joyful glee,
As raindrops fall, we skip with tea.
Nature's humor, light and bright,
Turns every storm into delight.

So let it rain, we'll dance away,
In this wild and wacky play.
With each drop that makes a sound,
A laughing heart is always found.

Sunsets Bathed in Tropical Hues

The skies alight in orange burst,
With pinks and purples, oh, the thirst!
As day gives way, the shadows creep,
While roosters crow, they've lost their sleep.

A hammock swings, a perfect spot,
As iguanas plot a daring trot.
The sun, a giant, melts away,
While crabs in sand take time to play.

With coconut drinks and straws so wide,
We toast to feasts and laughter's ride.
As evening paints the beach so bright,
The stars join in, what a sight!

So here's to sunsets from our chairs,
With crickets chirping all our cares.
When twilight falls, let giggles soar,
In colors bright, we laugh some more.

Nature's Symphony of Lush Sights

Bees buzz about, a drumming band,
While monkeys swing, their antics grand.
The trees clap hands in playful cheer,
As parrots squawk, "Come join us here!"

A lizard darts with speeds so fast,
While flowers bloom, a fragrant blast.
In every nook, a critter prance,
As snails take part in a slow dance.

Here laughter rings, in every sound,
The jungle's fun is always found.
Butterflies flutter, their colorful flair,
As frogs cheer on from lily square.

With nature's jokes, we'll not be sad,
In every laugh, a world so rad.
Join in the fun, the sights, the sounds,
In this lush symphony, joy abounds!

Hidden Gems of Vibrant Shores

On sandy shores, the crabs convene,
Conspiring in shadows, oh what a scene!
With flip-flops flying, it's a race,
While gulls swoop down to claim their space.

The waves tickle toes, a playful tease,
As sunbathers groan in sunburn's breeze.
A treasure hunt for seashells rare,
While fish flip-flop, causing a scare.

With every splash, a giggly cheer,
As dolphins join, they bring good cheer.
In vibrant hues, the sunsets flow,
Creating tales only the sea will know.

So grab your hats, and let's explore,
These hidden gems, oh what a score!
Adventures wait on vibrant shores,
Where laughter echoes, and fun restores.

The Spice of the Earth's Eden

In the market, fruits make a fuss,
Watermelons flaunt, they're all a plus.
Bananas talking gossip, quite a scene,
Who knew veggies held such a routine?

Coconut shells win hide-and-seek,
While mangoes giggle, oh so chic.
Pickles riding roller coasters of spice,
Jalapeños on a dance floor, oh so nice!

Lime slices hold a zesty debate,
Should they take the plunge, or just wait?
Herbs with ambitions to become a meal,
Chasing pigeons, what a surreal deal!

A feast of laughter, colors galore,
In this Eden, you'll never bore.
Let's spice it up with some fun and cheer,
Life's too short for a dull frontier!

Melodies of Motion in Stillness

The palm trees sway to a silent beat,
Twisting to rhythms that cannot be beat.
Chillin' like villains in the warmest breeze,
While the lazy wind whispers through the leaves.

A parrot raps with a cadence so sweet,
While iguanas mock with their slow-moving feet.
Mangoes are jamming on a tropical groove,
Swaying and swaying, just trying to move!

Coconuts chuckle, holding their ground,
With watermelon beats, they bounce all around.
In this dance of stillness, it's quite a sight,
Even the suns' rays join the delight!

Stars blink in sync, what a quirky show,
Crickets are crooning, putting on their glow.
Every creature joins in this light-hearted spree,
It's a festival of laughter, let's all agree!

A Kiss of Tropic Serenity

In the shade of the trees, a secret kiss,
A lizard sunbathing, pure bliss.
Sandals abandoned for some flip-flop fun,
Crabs in a race, oh, who will be done?

The sun winks down, a playful tease,
As waves whisper sweet nothings with ease.
A turtle drifts by, wearing shades so cool,
While fish swim in circles, in their own little pool.

Seagulls caw gossip, soaring high in the sky,
While palm leaves gossip, saying, "Oh my! Oh my!"
The coconuts hover, plotting a prank,
On unsuspecting tourists, how much they can prank!

Under this canopy, life dances slow,
With everything giggling, putting on a show.
It's a kiss of calm, with a wink of cheer,
Who knew serenity could be so dear?

Clandestine Wonder Beneath the Leaves

Under the foliage, secrets unwind,
Squirrels narrate stories that are one of a kind.
Bugs throw parties, bopping to the beat,
While ants form conga lines, oh so neat!

A snail in a shell, playing hide and seek,
With a funky dance, oh so unique.
Mushrooms giggle, shaking their caps,
Who knew fungi could pull such mishaps?

A frog's croak turns into a song,
While honeybees buzz, 'Hey, we belong!'
Beetles in tuxedos strut down the lane,
In this leafy haven, it's all quite insane!

Towers of leaves cradle secrets so sweet,
Nature's comedy show, what a treat!
Join the wild party, where laughter thrives,
In this clandestine shade, wonder thrives!

Golden Sands of Forgotten Shores

Waves giggle as they roll on by,
Shells whisper secrets, oh so sly.
Sunburnt tourists dance in sun,
Flip-flops lost, it's all good fun.

Seagulls squawk, like they know best,
While sandcastles survive the test.
Beach balls bounce like rubber ships,
Sandy toes and salty lips.

The sun sets low, a golden show,
Sandy snacks are all aglow.
Ice cream melts down children's chins,
As laughter spills where the day begins.

So grab your towel, join the cheer,
In this wild coast, there's naught to fear.
Surfboards dance upon the swell,
Join the party, oh do tell!

Reverence for Rain and Reeds

Pitter-patter, raindrops play,
Frogs are crooning, hip-hip-hooray!
Mud puddles scream, 'Come take a leap!',
All the critters stir from sleep.

Turtles waddle in the wet,
Singing songs, they're a funny set.
The reeds quiver, bow with grace,
As breezes play a game of chase.

The clouds burst forth, a drippy dance,
Umbrellas flip; who took that chance?
Splashing through is all the rage,
We're the stars upon this stage.

So rain away, dear skies of gray,
In this big splash, we laugh and play.
Join the chorus, sing along,
With nature's beat, we can't go wrong!

Flora's Flourish and Fauna's Flight

Blooms in colors loud and bright,
Dancing petals take their flight.
Bumblebees with cheer do hum,
While lizards prance—don't be so glum.

Monkeys swing from vine to vine,
Chasing shadows, feeling fine.
Parrots squawk in vivid tones,
While flowers sport their polka-dots and cones.

Butterflies in silly pairs,
Flutter forth without a care.
Ode to blooms and playful charms,
Nature's giggles fill our arms.

So laugh, dear friend, at life so grand,
In this wild mess, take a stand.
With every twist, there's joy in sight,
Together let's embrace this delight!

The Silver Stream of Lush Life

Rippling waters, cool and bright,
Frogs in chorus, a froggy fight.
Fish flash fins like glimmers spark,
As dragonflies buzz round the park.

Otters slip and slide with glee,
Rolling round like rascally spree.
With snacks of moss and splashes wide,
This bubbling brook can't be denied.

Nuts squirrel away, slow poke style,
While water lilies wear a smile.
The stream laughs softly with the breeze,
Join the fun beneath the trees.

So brew your tea beside this flow,
Nature's antics put on a show.
Bring your pals, let's play the day,
In this lush life, we'll dance away!

Wild Pulses of Nature's Beat

In the jungle, monkeys chatter,
Lizards dance on leaves that scatter.
Parrots squawk a tune so bright,
While sloths move slow, what a sight!

Coconuts drop with a thud,
And ants march on like a flood.
Bees are buzzing, here and there,
It's a party—who needs air?

Colorful blooms in laughter sing,
While frogs leap in a daring fling.
With every splash, the fun increases,
Nature's joy never ceases!

Flora's Dance in Humid Embrace

In the mist, plants sway and twist,
Even cacti can't resist.
Vines lounge like they own the place,
They share with trees a leafy grace.

Fern fronds do a jig so spry,
While flowers wink as bees pass by.
Petals flutter, dressed so fine,
Join the rhythm, sip the wine!

Bamboo flutes play tunes so sweet,
Palm leaves tap, it's quite the feat.
In this party nature planned,
Everyone's got a dance to stand!

Where the Ocean Meets the Forest

The waves crash in with a giggle,
While crabs dance a funny wiggle.
Seagulls soar with silly calls,
Bounding on the beach, oh what thralls!

Driftwood lounges like it's on break,
Rocky formations ready to shake.
Coconuts roll like they're playing tag,
While the wind gives nature a wag.

Tangled roots stretch, waving hello,
Fish peek out in a vibrant show.
Together they frolic, it's a blast,
Under the sun, shadows cast!

The Tides of Time in Warm Breezes

The clock ticks slow, like turtles crawl,
In this paradise, we hear the call.
Time's just a suggestion, you see,
As we sip on fresh coconut tea.

Breezes giggle with tales from afar,
Carrying secrets of each star.
Even the sunset wears a grin,
While nightfall awakens a joyful din.

Fireflies flicker, a natural show,
Their tiny lights dance to and fro.
With laughter echoing through the trees,
Every moment's a breeze of ease!

www.ingramcontent.com/pod-product-compliance
Lightning Source LLC
Chambersburg PA
CBHW072129070526
44585CB00016B/1601